Dissertation Writing: The Easy Way!

What it Takes to Finish a Dissertation, Dissertation Sections and Section Length
Requirements, and Reaping the Rewards of Earning a Doctorate Degree

Peggy M. Houghton, Ph.D.
Timothy J. Houghton, Ph.D.
Edited by Pamela A. Presnal

Outline of Handbook

This quick and easy-to-read handbook is divided into three sections. The section title as well as the parts included is as follows:

Section One: Yes...You Can Do It!

Making it Happen

Writing a dissertation is a long, arduous task...no doubt about it. However, we are here to prove to you that it is a very real and achievable goal. We're living proof! In fact, 50 percent of our immediate family members have doctorate degrees. The authors of this book are siblings (not husband and wife as many of our readers believe!). We, along with our mother, all have doctorate degrees. Our mother completed her degree at the age of fifty-seven. We were a tad younger, 38 and 31 respectively. Trust us, it can be done!

Was the task difficult? Did we sacrifice time with family and friends? Did we have sleepless nights? Was the dissertation process demanding and time-consuming? Did we maintain full-time employment? As you might expect, the answer to these questions is a resounding yes. However, there is nothing that can't be accomplished without support, discipline, and perseverance. Enough about us, let's talk about how you will succeed!

Support Structure

There is no question about it...you need the support of your family (primarily), colleagues, and friends.

Support and encouragement from your spouse, significant other, children, etc. is essential. Just as you will have to sacrifice things in life, they too will have to do the same. This is a joint effort that requires buy-in from all who might be affected by the dedicated time required to successfully complete the doctoral journey.

An added bonus is when your employer is providing encouragement along the way as well. It's even better if your employer provides some type of incentive for higher education. This may be in the form of tuition and/or textbook assistance, additional paid time off work to study, or potential career advancement upon completion of advanced degree.

After you've secured the necessary support...it's time for you to get disciplined!

Discipline

This is where you come into play. You are the one who is ultimately responsible for your future. As such, you need to be regimentally disciplined in order to successfully finalize your dissertation.

After years of serving on all types of dissertation committees, we have come to the conclusion that students can become all-consumed and overwhelmed at the macro level. In other words, they think of the dissertation as an impossible task that is simply not achievable.

How, then, can the dissertation be finalized? How can this seemingly undoable final product come to fruition? We are strong advocates of *chunking* tasks that appear on the surface to be insurmountable.

As the name implies, *chunking* merely divides, or chunks, a large task into several small components. Take, for example, chapter one of the dissertation. You may find that the chapter consists of 10-15 different sections. Map out a plan by chunking out the various elements. For example, you may decide to take one section per day. Set aside time each day to research and write on only that particular section. Be diligent and disciplined with respect to your time allocation. Motivate yourself to sit down and write. While this can be difficult at times, completion of a section provides a real sense of accomplishment!

Perseverance

Discipline and perseverance go hand and hand. In order to succeed, you will need to work relentlessly on the dissertation process. As noted in the discipline section, you must judiciously dedicate daily time to the writing process. Procrastination can easily creep into your daily schedule, but you must be persistent and ward off the procrastination temptation.

Many students possess the discipline, perseverance, and tenacity to complete the course work required to obtain a doctorate degree. However, they simply can't make it to the finish line...the completion of the written dissertation. These students are lumped into a category labeled ABD (All But Dissertation). The Council of Graduate Studies cites some very alarming statistics. According to Smallwood and the Workshop on Graduate School Attrition (as cited in Council of Graduate Schools, 2014, para. 1):

> Despite recent national attention focusing on doctoral completion, the Analysis of Baseline Program Data from the Ph.D. Completion Project, which examined both private and public institutions nationally, reports that the completion rate ten years after students begin their doctoral program remains low at 56.6% (Sowell, Zhang, Redd, & King, 2008). Additionally, the analysis indicates that completion rates continue to vary considerably by field of study: 49.3% in humanities, 54.7% in mathematics and physical sciences, 55.9% in social sciences, 62.9% in life sciences, and 63.6% in engineering. Such low completion rates result in concerns ranging from the waste of limited resources and our "domestic talent pool," to the detrimental effects on students' lives (Smallwood, 2004; Workshop on Graduate School Attrition, 1997).

The *All But Dissertation* status is a costly status, not only for the student but also for the Academic Institution and society at large. The pursuit of a doctorate degree is a very expensive endeavor. As was noted previously, doctoral students make substantial financial sacrifices as well as personal sacrifices while pursuing a degree. The College or University in which the student attends also makes a financial commitment. Time involved with recruiting, enrolling, mentoring, and teaching essentially was done in vain since the degree is not ultimately conferred. Finally, society as a whole also loses. There is one less scholar practitioner making a difference by contributing newly gained knowledge pertaining to a current gap in existing literature.

Having said this, it's obvious that the final phase of the doctoral journey, or the completed dissertation, is a must to make an educational dream come to completion. In the end, a published dissertation is well worth the discipline and perseverance that was demonstrated throughout the arduous process. Your support system will reap rewards as well!

Enough said...let's talk about what's involved!

Section Two: Common Elements Required in Most Dissertations...The "What's Included" and General Number of Pages for Each Section.

Special Note: Every academic Institution will mandate specific elements required in each chapter of their respective dissertation. As such, the authors of this handbook chose to take a generic approach to listing and providing an approximate length of the elements included in a common five-chapter dissertation. In some instances, the explanation for each element is further clarified using examples as support.

It's important to realize, however, that this is a generic explanation of what's included in a common five-chapter dissertation. Be sure to review your academic Institution's specific requirements and adjust your writing accordingly.

Additionally, an approximate writing length for each section is included (*highlighted in red font*).

Title Page

The title page is very simple, but it does vary from institution to institution. Essentially it contains the following:

- Title
- Author (full name)
- Date (year only)
- Degree and Major
- University
- Advisor

Length - All information for the title page should be contained on one page.

Copyright Page (optional)

The copyright page provides copyright protection of your work. Essentially it contains the following:

- Copyright symbol (©)
- Author (full name)
- Date (year only)
- All Rights Reserved

Acknowledgements or Dedication Page (optional)

The acknowledgements or dedication page gives credit to the people who helped or supported the author throughout the dissertation process. It typically includes advisors, committee members, fellow students, coworkers, family, and/or friends.

Abstract

The abstract is optional at some universities, but essentially it is a condensed summary of the dissertation. Keep in mind that it is a description of your work that often functions as the determining factor as to whether or not potential readers will continue on and read the full text.

The abstract should:

- Summarize the research problem
- Summarize the research design and procedure
- Summarize the significant results

The abstract should not:

- Include abbreviations or acronyms that were not first identified
- Include reference citations

Table of Contents

The table of contents provides a list of the parts of the dissertation in the order that they appear. Essentially it should list headings and page numbers.

List of Tables and Figures

The list of tables and figures provides a list of the tables and figures in the order they appear. Essentially it should list textual information and numerical data that is presented in a column.

Length – A list of tables uses as many pages as required to contain all of the necessary information. Obviously, more tables and figures require more pages.

Chapter One: Introduction

To begin, chapter one generally consists of the following components:

- Introduction
- Problem Statement
- Problem Background
- Purpose of the Study
- Theoretical Support
- Assumptions
- Scope and Delimitations
- Limitations
- Nature of the Study
- Definition of Terms
- Research Questions and/or Hypotheses
- Significance of the Study
- Summary

A brief description of each section as well as an approximate length of the section follows:

Introduction

The introduction should provide a brief explanation regarding the basic interest of the study. The problem should be stated as well, in addition to a cursory review of supporting literature. You should explicitly state what the study results will attempt to accomplish.

Length – 1-3 pages

Problem Statement

Defining the problem statement is generally the most difficult task of a dissertation. While you may have an idea what you would like to study, oftentimes it's difficult to state accurately and succinctly.

The problem statement should be a one-sentence problem that has not yet been studied. Similar existing literature should be available to enhance the topic, but your study should be unique and fill a gap or void in existing data.

Most doctoral candidates have a problem statement that is broad and general. Generally speaking, a "funnel" technique should be used that starts with a broad overview and gradually narrows to the actual problem. Consider the following examples with **the problem statement italicized and underlined**:

Problem Statement (Example #1):

The careers people choose are influenced by various aspects of their lives. Experiences help them establish their identity and move through life into jobs that progress over many years. Famous people are also influenced by experiences, but their experiences are particularly interesting due to their public persona and the fact that they are often household names. *It is well known that these actors are famous, but the influences that inspired them to reach that status are often not understood.*

Problem Statement (Example #2):

Human beings interact with each other throughout their lives on personal and professional levels. Personal relationships are important, but they can be chosen by the individuals involved. People do not always get to choose who they work with; and, for this reason, workplace relationships tend to be more important than personal relationships. Spending eight or more hours a day at work with the same basic group of individuals can lead to stressful situations, and people sometimes attack each other verbally in order to get others to comply with their ideas, thinking, or beliefs. This type of verbally aggressive behavior often has negative effects. *In fact, verbal aggressiveness in the workplace results in many problems that adversely affect productivity.*

Length – ½-1 page

Problem Background

The problem background should include information that currently exists related to the problem statement for your particular study. There should be substantial existing background evidence to the issue under study, yet your specific problem should fill a gap, or void, that currently exists with existing data. A brief summary of major findings pertaining to the study should be included.

Length – 1-3 pages

Purpose of the Study

As with the problem statement, the purpose of the study clearly and distinctly explains the purpose, or *what,* your study is attempting to accomplish. The primary goal of this section is to state the desired goal of the study. Additionally, the importance of the study or reasons as to "why" the study is relevant should also be identified.

Length – ½-1 page

Theoretical Support

Theoretical support of a study includes existing theories and empirical research that lend credence to your proposed study. Your specific research problem should be unique and fill a void or gap, but existing literature should be provided as a basis for the foundational structure of your study. A theoretical framework provides the foundation for a solid study based on existing research and empirical data. ***Portions of a theoretical support section are provided below:***

Theoretical Support (Example #1):

One thing many famous people have in common is the fact that they established goals and made concerted efforts to achieve them. This follows Lock's (1968) Goal-Setting Theory with the thinking that motivation is driven by setting goals rather than just "doing your best." Taylor and Jones (2014) noted famous people often put their career in front of everything else because they are so compelled to succeed.

Success can be defined in many different ways, but Wyman (2001) found that famous people believe success is a direct measure of career achievement. Consequently, family and personal lives typically are not as important as work. Other research (Watts & Wood, 2006) indicates famous people value success over fame, and they see fame as an after effect of success that they have little control over. Jagger and Richards (2014) also found fame to be something that could not be controlled, and it has a positive and negative impact on famous people's lives.

Theoretical Support (Example #2):

Verbal aggressiveness is defined as behavior using a personal and psychological assault on an individual's mental well-being during human interaction (Visconti, 2013). Victims of verbal aggressiveness are generally led to think less favorably about themselves (Gudykunst, Ting-Toomey, Sudweeks, & Stewart, 1995; Infante & Wigley, 1986), and negative interpersonal relationships can develop. The effects of verbal aggression are rarely positive.

Verbal aggressiveness has many forms, and it is not limited to face-to-face interaction. A destructive message can be delivered through other means. Telephones, fax machines, and computers are all mediums available for personal attacks (Quietkowski, 2012). Kiesler and Sproull (1992) indicated that, compared to face-to-face discussion, computer mediated discussion leads to more frequent and deeper verbal aggressiveness in the form of "flaming."

Dubrovsky, Kiesler, and Sethna (1991) found that one group of people made more than eight times as many "flaming" remarks in 24 electronic discussions than they did in the same number of face-to-face discussions.

Length – 4-10 pages

Assumptions

Assumptions are things you, as the writer, take for granted. They must be stated to the reader to provide credibility and validity to the study.

There are usually general as well as specific study assumptions identified by the researcher. Assumptions might include such things as the willingness of participants to engage in the study, honesty of participants, whether or not the sample size is reflective of the desired population, etc.

Assumptions should not only be stated, but addressed. For example, you may wish to discuss the consent form that allows for participant anonymity and confidentiality. To assume that the sample group is appropriate for the study, a pilot study might be implemented. It is important to remember, however, that participants who are utilized in the pilot study cannot be part of the actual study.

Length – ½-1 page

Scope and Delimitations

The scope and delimitations are generally listed in the same section of the dissertation document. Again, these elements are cited to lend credibility to the study.

Specifically, the scope of the study includes the overall boundaries of the study. The scope generally narrows your research topic and more succinctly describes elements of the study. It might include such things as who or what will be studied, the geographical location in which the study will take place, the timeframe of the study, etc. These descriptors indicate the breadth of the study.

Delimitations further explain the scope of the study. This particular section might include such things as why a particular group or thing was chosen, why a particular group or thing was excluded, specific variables of the study, etc. Essentially, they are constraints imposed by the researcher.

Length – 1-3 pages

Limitations

Limitations are things in the study that simply cannot be controlled by the researcher. However, limitations should always be clearly stated to add credibility to the study. Examples of limitations might include such things as the following:

- Number of participants included in the study. Is the sample selection appropriate to state that the results are representative of the entire population?
- Generalizability of the study results. In other words, can the results of the study be considered appropriate for other geographical areas, demographic changes, etc.?
- Does the writer hold any biases toward the topic being studied?
- Does the writer possess preconceived notions of the results of the study prior to conducting the research?

Again, limitations of the study must be identified and openly stated.

Length – 1-2 pages

Nature of the Study

This section provides a brief introduction as to the design of the study. The design generally will fall under one of three categories: quantitative, qualitative, or mixed-methods. A mixed methods approach is essentially a combination of both quantitative and qualitative designs. You should mention which design will be utilized for your study and provide rationale as to why this design is appropriate for the study.

A more detailed discussion of the research design is explained in chapter three.

Length – ½-1 page

Definition of Terms

The definition of terms section should be considered a "work-in-progress" portion since the terms will undoubtedly grow as the study advances. However, this section should include all terms used throughout the study that are not considered "common knowledge" by the average reader.

The terms should be operationally defined; that is, they should be defined with regard to how they are used within the study. Terms should be listed and defined with appropriate credit granted to the defining source. In addition to terms, all acronyms should be listed and defined.

Length – 1-4 pages

Research Questions and/or Hypotheses

Research questions or hypotheses are used based on the design of the study.

Research questions, as implied by the name, ask a specific question related to the study. They are always written as a question and are generally used with qualitative studies. The following are examples of research questions:

1. What situations influenced famous actors?
2. What people influenced famous actors?
3. What events influenced famous actors?

Hypotheses are statements regarding the relationship between two or more variables. An accurately stated hypothesis includes three elements: the variables being studied, the population under study, and the relationship between the variables. Hypotheses are tested by rejecting null hypotheses, and they are generally used with quantitative studies. The following is an example of a hypothesis as well as a null hypothesis:

Hypothesis (Example #1):

In organizational interaction, increasing target perception of verbal aggressiveness (independent variable) will be correlated with decreasing target organizational commitment (dependent variable).

Null Hypothesis (Example #2):

In organizational interaction, increasing target perception of verbal aggressiveness (independent variable) will not be correlated with decreasing target organizational commitment (dependent variable).

Length – ½-1 page

Significance of the Study

The significance of the study includes such things as why the study is important, who/what might benefit from the study, the contribution to existing data, etc. This section should explain how the proposed new data will complement and strengthen existing data.

Length – 1-2 pages

Summary

The summary is a brief conclusion of what was included in chapter one. Do not simply repeat what was written, rather provide a general synopsis of the content. Additionally, make a logical transition into chapter two of the document. Provide a brief overview of the elements of chapter two.

Length – 1-3 paragraphs

Chapter Two: Literature Review

Chapter Two minimally consists of the following components:

- Introduction
- Theoretical or Conceptual Framework of Literature
- Summary

Introduction

The introduction of this chapter should provide a framework as to how the chapter will be developed and organized. Foundational theories and concepts that substantiate the proposed study should be briefly noted. Why are these important? How do they enhance and strengthen the study?

The introduction can be strengthened by providing a literature map to guide the reader through the organization of the chapter. A simple search on any popular Internet Search Engine will provide an abundance of examples as well as detailed templates to utilize with the development of a literature map.

Length – ½-2 pages

Theoretical or Conceptual Framework of Literature

This is the "meat" of the section. It includes a ***comprehensive*** review of the literature related to your specific research problem, research questions, and the methodology being utilized. It should demonstrate knowledge of the dissertation topic, analyze existing related research, and synthesize the research as it pertains to the specific topic under study.

Similar to the development of the problem statement, a "funnel approach" is commonly used with this section. Essentially, this type of approach involves beginning with broad existing literature and then narrowing the literature to specific foundations/concepts that relate to your particular study. The funnel approach begins very broad in scope and gradually narrows to literature that is truly relevant to your topic. Keep in mind, however, that this is a thorough review and should be written accordingly.

As with the literature map, there are multiple websites and templates of literature reviews utilizing the funnel method located on the Internet. These are very detailed and provide many examples. We strongly encourage a review of these various examples as they will be very beneficial with the completion of the literature review writing.

Length – Dependent on the complexity of the study, this section is generally 15-30 pages.

Summary

This section highlights the major points mentioned in the chapter. It includes a summary of what has been discussed as well as a brief introduction to the next chapter.

Length – ½-1 page

Chapter Three: Methodology

Chapter three generally consists of the following components:

- Introduction
- Research Design
- Population
- Sampling Method
- Sample Selection
- Instrumentation
- Data Collection
- Data Analysis
- Researcher Role
- Human Participant Protection
- Summary

Introduction

As with most introductions, this section is relatively brief. The intent of the section is to provide the reader with an overview of the chapter. It should list the various elements that will be discussed.

Length – ¼-1 page

Research Design

This section states what type of research design will be utilized with the study. It is the strategy employed to effectively attempt to answer your research questions. There are generally three types of design...qualitative, quantitative, and mixed-methods.

Qualitative research is used to study human behavior, while quantitative research is implemented to statistically analyze and measure the way in which people think, feel, or behave. Phenomenological, ethnographic, grounded theory, and case study are examples of design that might be considered for a qualitative study. Quantitative research, on the on the other hand, includes such things as experimental, correlational, survey, or secondary data analysis. Finally, mixed-methods, as the name implies, is a combination of both quantitative and qualitative design. Again, an Internet search will provide an in-depth learning experience regarding the various types of research design.

You will need to state which design method you have selected for the study and provide rationale as to why this was specifically selected. Since there may likely be multiple types that could be utilized, you should clearly indicate why the chosen type is the most appropriate for your study.

Length – 2-3 pages

Population

This section describes the overall potential population for the study. It might include such things as an entire group of people, events, households, etc. This is obviously dependent upon the study. When determining your specific study, you should have a clear understanding of who or what the entire population could potentially include. Given time, financial, and other obvious constraints, the entire population is almost never used in any given study. We hesitate to say never, as in rare cases this may be possible. It is critical to define the characteristics of the population, since future researchers may wish to pursue a different study using the same population...but a different sample group. At any rate, the population is the entire entity of which the sample will be chosen.

Length – ½-1 page

Sampling Method

The sampling method is used to determine the sample group that will be utilized for your study. Sampling types are generally defined as either probability or nonprobability   Examples of probability sampling methods include simple random, stratified, cluster, and systematic. Alternatively, some examples of nonprobability sampling methods include convenience, quota, purposive, and snowball. Again, a simple search on the Internet will provide a further explanation of the various sampling methods as well as supply a multitude of potential examples.

The sampling method section should include the type of method, why this particular method is appropriate for the given study, and the sample frame (a list of all those in a population who could potentially be sampled).

Length – ½ - 1 page

Sample Selection

This section describes the sample, or selected portion, to be part of the study. As the name implies, it is a portion or subset of the population and is determined by the selected sampling method. These are the specific people, events, households, etc. that will be included in the study.

Characteristics and/or demographics of the sample should be identified. The rationale for selecting this sample size must be explained and justified. Is the sample an appropriate representation of the sampling frame? What percentage of the population was selected for your study? Is this particular sample representative of the larger population?

The sample selection is a critical component of the dissertation. If properly selected, it can allow for study results to be generalized to the larger population.

Length – ½-1 page

Instrumentation

The instrumentation explains the device being utilized to collect your data. Examples might include such things as the following:

- Surveys
- Questionnaires
- Interviews
- Case Studies
- Ethnography
- Experimental Research
- Observation

The instrumentation device allows the researcher to compile and describe observed data. The chosen device should be identified and explained. Additionally, rationale for its selection should be provided.

Length –1-3 pages

Data Collection

The data collection is the "meat and potatoes" of the study. This is when the researcher digs deep into the trenches and begins to seek out data specific to the study. Based upon the chosen instrumentation, data collection results in a systematic process that enables the researcher to acquire required data to answer the stated research questions and finalize the study.

For example, when conducting observations, defining what is being observed as well as the rationale for conducting observations at the appropriate times must be provided. The observations should be recorded and organized in the most effective manner possible. Likewise, if questionnaires are used, will they be electronic? Will they be mailed (and will return postage be provided)? What are the time restrictions to complete the form, etc.?

Regardless of whether human participants are being utilized, generally an IRB (Institutional Review Board) request must be completed and submitted (see *Protection of Human Participants* section below). This submission protects the rights and welfare of study participants. Some studies may require a consent form. The researcher should consult with the Institution for specific guidelines regarding the IRB process.

Length – 2-5 pages

Data Analysis

Once the data has been collected, it must be analyzed. Analyzing the data involves a thorough review of the collected information. By examining the data, the researcher attempts to identify potential themes, patterns, or trends that have occurred throughout the data collection. These various themes, patterns, or trends revealed are then compared to a control variable (group, figure, occupation, etc.) to help draw conclusions from the data collected by the researcher.

There are essentially two types of data...qualitative and quantitative. As previously noted, sometimes both qualitative and quantitative data is utilized. This is considered a mixed methods study. If independently used, however, qualitative data consists of "soft" data or things that might be perceived, observed, interpreted, etc. While this may be considered a weakness in that bias may be intentionally or unintentionally injected, in actuality, it can provide a rich source of analysis. Certain perceptions, observations, interpretations, etc. simply cannot be translated into numeric format. Thus, based on the type of study, qualitative analysis may well be the appropriate research method to be utilized.

Quantitative data involves the use of numbers. Scores, percentages, and satisfaction rates are examples of quantitative data. Statistical processes such as calculating the mean or average number of times an event occurs (per day, month, year, etc.) are generally a function of qualitative data. Since this type of "hard" data is utilized, a more definitive and less subjective analysis sometimes prevails. These operations, because numbers are "hard" data and not subject to interpretation, can give relatively definitive answers to different questions.

The data type should be dependent on the study under investigation. Regardless of the chosen data type, the analysis section includes a detailed review of the collected information. The analysis should be presented in a logical, clear format. You should describe the process as to how the data will be analyzed and presented.

Length – 2-5 pages

Researcher Role

Regardless of the type of study, an explanation of the researcher's role is necessary. Declaring the role of the researcher exposes any type of bias that may result during the study. Biases can intentionally or unintentionally occur for a multitude of reasons. For example, a qualitative study design might include surveying participants. Is the researcher familiar with the research participants? Are the participants selected by the researcher? Will participant responses be published in the study? The answers to these questions may indicate a researcher bias.

Likewise, a quantitative study can also present biases. Take, for example, a questionnaire. Are the participants subordinates or supervisors to the researcher? Could participant responses tarnish their respective careers? Will participant responses have a bearing on merit increases? Again, the answers might indicate a potential bias on the part of the researcher.

There are many possibilities that could result in a bias of the study and thus result in skewed results. Therefore, the specific role of the researcher must be identified and declared so that the reader is fully aware of any potential prejudices that may surface.

Length – ½-1 page

Protection of Human Participants

As noted in the *Data Collection* section, regardless of whether human participants are being utilized, generally an IRB (Institutional Review Board) request form must be completed and submitted. This submission protects the rights and welfare of study participants.

Even after the IRB form is submitted and approved, the researcher must specify in the actual paper what will be completed to protect and ensure all participants' rights. The following are a few questions that might be addressed in any IRB submission:

- In what way will the research be conducted so as to protect the rights and privacy of the participants?
- How will the confidentiality of the participants be preserved?
- How will the data collection process not cause anxiety or harm to the participants?

Some studies may require a consent form. The researcher should consult with the Institution for specific guidelines regarding the IRB process.

18

Length – ½-1 page

Summary

The summary of the chapter provides a sense of chapter closure. While a relatively brief section, the researcher should make mention of the key components of the chapter. Also, a few paragraphs summarizing the emerging themes, patterns, or trends that have occurred during the data analysis as well as any other significant or interesting findings discovered during the process should be noted. You should finalize the chapter with a brief introduction to chapter four.

Length – ½-1 page

Chapter Four: Results

Chapter Four conveys the actual results of the study.

- Qualitative Research Reporting
- Quantitative Research Reporting

The results section presents the findings from the data gathered by the researcher in a manner that is easily understood. It is important to remember that the findings are presented in the results, not interpreted. Findings are interpreted in Chapter Five (*Summary, Recommendations, and Conclusions*).

The dissertation design type determines the nature of the findings presentation. Results from qualitative studies are generally reported differently than those of quantitative studies. Chapter four of a qualitative dissertation is usually longer than that of a quantitative dissertation because quantitative reporting is in tabular or numerical format and does not require as much description.

Qualitative Research Reporting

The introduction to qualitative research reporting revisits the purpose of the study. It should be one or two paragraphs that transition well into the results reporting.

Next begin the reporting of the research. First, define the demographics of the research. Include age, race, gender, sexual orientation, or other important information as it relates to the population. Tables and illustrations can be used for better description and/or clarification.

Next, go into the findings of the research and highlight the salient aspects. There is no exact way to do this, but one method involves extracting patterns derived from the data. Present these patterns as units of qualitative measurement. For example, a unit of qualitative measurement for a study involving interviews of famous actors might be specific timeframes of their lives listed in chronological order.

Assume a unit of qualitative measure, or pattern, is the famous actors' youth. Using their interview responses, look for sub-patterns within that pattern. If the famous actors consistently related back to their grandmothers for inspiration when answering questions about their youth, then this is a sub-pattern that should be noted.

Also add outliers to the analysis. Outliers are distinctly different data from the vast majority of data collected. They are important because they can indicate a pattern or sub-pattern that is difficult to notice. If the famous actors only mentioned school once as inspiration when answering questions about their youth, then this should be noted as an outlier. The point is to dig deeper in order to find patterns or sub-patterns that might normally be missed.

The last portion of qualitative research reporting should summarize the emerging patterns. Keep in mind that chapter four presents the findings, but does not discuss their importance. Chapter five evaluates and interprets the findings and discusses their significance. Additionally, do not compare the finding discussed in chapter four with similarities in related literature because that should have already been completed in the literature review section (chapter two) of the dissertation.

Total Qualitative Length 15-20 pages

Quantitative Research Reporting

The introduction to quantitative research reporting revisits the purpose of the study. It should be one or two paragraphs that transition well into the results reporting.

Next begin the reporting of the research. First, define the demographics of the research. Include age, race, gender, sexual orientation, or other important information as it relates to the population. Tables and illustrations can be used for better description and/or clarification.

Next, describe the methods for data collection and note the tests, tables, graphs, and illustrations used. Discuss the instruments used to collect the data along with any databases that were drawn upon. If a survey is used, note the number of survey respondents and the number of incomplete surveys. Make certain that the methodology used matches that in Chapter Three (*Methodology*). If it does not, then the dissertation is not credible.

Assume the survey is looking for a correlation between two variables, and one hypothesis predicted that there would be a relationship. Revisit that hypothesis and describe what the survey found. Discuss the mean scores, standard deviations, and results of the Pearson's r Correlational Coefficient or ANOVA. In other words, show what happened and how it relates to the hypothesis. Also revisit the validity and reliability of the survey used to assure the reader that it was legitimate for the research.

Remember to report missing data. If data mentioned in Chapter Three (*Methodology*) could not be collected, then explain the reason why. For example, the research might have been designed to collect 100 surveys. However, after sending out 250 surveys, only 75 were returned. Management of the organization being surveyed wanted the process to stop because it was hindering employees' work, so discuss the fact that the survey had to be based on 75 respondents.

The last paragraph of quantitative research reporting should summarize the results in order of significance. Keep in mind that chapter four presents the findings, but does not discuss their importance. Chapter five evaluates and interprets the findings and discusses their significance. Additionally, do not compare the finding discussed in chapter four with similarities in related literature because that should have already been done in the literature review section (chapter two) of the dissertation.

Total Quantitative – 10-20 pages

Chapter Five: Summary, Recommendations, and Conclusions

Chapter Five (*Summary, Recommendations, and Conclusions*) interprets the results from Chapter Four (*Results*).

- Qualitative Research Summary
- Qualitative Research Recommendations
- Qualitative Research Conclusion
- Quantitative Research Summary
- Quantitative Research Recommendations
- Quantitative Research Conclusion

The objective of this chapter is to discuss the importance of the findings, make recommendations for how the findings can be applied, and suggest ideas for future research. Always discuss the findings in the same order as Chapter Four (*Results*). This makes the flow easier to follow for the reader.

Qualitative Research Summary

The introduction to the qualitative research summary consists of one or two paragraphs that lead into the discussion section by revisiting the purpose of the study. The reader should be reminded why the research was conducted. Additionally, the research questions or hypotheses that guided the study should be included.

Begin the discussion by summarizing the results in chapter four and then note the reasons why those results are important. For example, if famous actors consistently indicated their ability to play musical instruments opened doors for their acting careers, then this is important because aspiring actors might start playing musical instruments in the hope that this will provide them with career opportunities.

Make sure the discussion section does not contradict or lack a relationship with the information from chapter four. If the famous actors talked about their grandmothers as being inspirational, then do not discuss the significance of their grandparents in their lives. There must be a smooth transition from the results to the discussion, and it must make sense.

A major goal of the discussion is to report patterns in the results that were not found in any other research. These patterns should then be expanded upon, and their importance or significance should be highlighted. If a pattern indicates the famous actors had older siblings who were on the debate team in high school, then this might be something that was not known before. Expand upon the significance of this new finding by making reasonable inferences. For example, watching their siblings practice debate at home might have impacted the famous actors desire to perform publicly.

Essentially, the discussion section of chapter five should be looking for answers to the following three major questions:

- Why are these findings significant?
- Who will benefit from these findings?
- How do these findings differ from previous research?

End the discussion with a paragraph that summarizes the significance of the major findings/patterns and transitions well into the recommendations section.

Qualitative Research Recommendations

The qualitative research recommendations section suggests how, where, and when the findings of the study can be applied. This section also discusses limitations of the study and generates ideas for future research.

Consider the potential study on famous actors. For example, maybe the recommendation section might begin by noting that these actors are under mental stress to remain popular in the public eye. They might only be remembered for their last performance...and that performance might not have been their best. This leads into the suggestion that psychologists who treat famous actors can benefit from the study because they will have a better understanding of the influences and inspirations of their lives.

Lastly, suggest some ideas for future research. Other doctoral students or researchers might want to expand upon this work with their own research. They could interview parents and siblings of famous people to see if they find patterns with their education, careers, hobbies, and lifestyles. They might also research something that was not a pattern.

Qualitative Research Conclusion

End with a paragraph or two that summarizes chapter five without adding any additional findings or making any new inferences. Briefly discuss the importance of the findings, the benefactors of the study, and future research suggestions.

Total Qualitative Length (Summary, Recommendations, and Conclusion) 15-20 pages

Quantitative Research Summary

The introduction to the quantitative research summary consists of one or two paragraphs that lead into the discussion section by revisiting the purpose of the study. The reader should be reminded why the research was conducted. Additionally, the research questions or hypotheses that guided the study should be included.

Begin the discussion by summarizing the results in chapter four and then note the reasons why those results are important. For example, if a survey results from an organizational study found that supervisor verbal aggressiveness results in increased employee absenteeism, then this is important to leaders of organizations who want to reduce employee absenteeism.

Explain whether or not the findings supported each research question or hypothesis and note if the relationships are consistent with traditional thinking. Be sure not to contradict a relationship or lack of relationship with the information from chapter four. For example, if verbal aggressiveness did not have a negative impact on employee motivation, then do not discuss a correlation between the two variables. There must be a smooth transition from the results to the discussion, and it must make sense.

A major goal of the discussion is to report results that were not found in any other research. These findings should then be expanded upon, and their importance or significance highlighted. If there was a correlation between verbal aggressiveness and organizational commitment, then this might be something that was not known before. Expand upon the significance of this new finding by making reasonable inferences. For example, reducing verbal aggressiveness might result in employees being more committed to organizational goals resulting in increased productivity.

Essentially, the discussion section of chapter five should be looking for answers to the following three major questions:

- Why are these findings significant?
- Who will benefit from these findings?
- How do these findings differ from previous research?

End the discussion with a paragraph that summarizes the significance of the major findings/patterns and transitions well into the recommendations section.

Quantitative Research Recommendations

The quantitative research recommendations section suggests how, where, and when the findings of the study can be applied.

Consider the example pertaining to verbal aggressiveness. Leadership in organizations can benefit from the findings because they can use them to reduce employee absenteeism. Additionally, this study can be used to further educational research. Theory and practical application fuel each other in the ever-changing global marketplace, and education is the key for developing new ways for organizations to become more competitive.

Finally, suggest some ideas for future research. Other doctoral students or researchers might want to expand upon this work with their own research. Gender might be a factor. Studies could investigate different organizational mixes of male and female subjects to find how they react to verbal aggressiveness. Another study could examine the impact of verbal aggressiveness in personal relationships. People might react differently to verbal attacks from family or close friends than they do to those from coworkers. There are a myriad of opportunities that exist for future research in any given study, and some potential possibilities should be identified in this section.

Quantitative Research Conclusions

End with a paragraph or two that summarizes chapter five without adding any additional findings or making any new inferences. Briefly discuss the importance of the findings, the benefactors of the study, and future research suggestions.

Total Quantitative Length (Summary, Recommendations, and Conclusion) 13-20 pages

Section Three: Finally Done...Reaping the Rewards!

Now I'm Done...What's Next? Let's consider some options!

Teaching

College teaching is probably the most desirable type of employment for people possessing doctoral degrees. One reason for this is the fact that most professor positions (both full and part time) require a doctorate. Another reason is because doctoral graduates understand academia well because they spent so many years in the system. They start at the bottom of the academic ladder, as an entry level freshman, and work their way up to the top rung, or professor status, after they receive their doctorate.

College professors' professional job descriptions vary from institution to institution. This is because universities and colleges emphasize different aspects of academia...and so do their respective professors. Some professors focus on teaching, some accentuate research, and still others work toward advancing into an administrative capacity.

Other professors like to conduct research. They do this so they can publish scholarly articles or books. Sometimes these publications are necessary in order to keep their tenured positions; this is how the phrase "publish or perish" came to fruition.

Regardless of the specific path chosen, a career in higher education will likely involve teaching at some point. College administrators generally mandate that their doctoral level courses be taught by faculty who have earned doctoral degrees from accredited Institutions. A master's degree might meet the minimum requirement, but students and accrediting bodies prefer a doctorate in most instances.

Teaching can be broken down into two basic types...traditional (brick and mortar) and virtual (online).

In the traditional classroom, instructors typically need to live within about a 50 mile radius of the institution. This is simply because a round trip commute greater than 100 miles makes most people question whether the job is worth the two hours per day spent driving.

The virtual classroom provides an even greater opportunity for those possessing a doctoral degree. Commutes are irrelevant in the online environment. Teachers do not have to go to a physical building, so the pool of applicants for teaching positions is worldwide. As long as the instructor has Internet access, he or she can live anywhere in the world and teach an online course. For this reason, online academic institutions are beginning to require doctoral degrees for teaching jobs at all levels. Those who possess only a master's degree are weeded out before the instructor search begins.

Consulting

People with doctorates spent a lot of time, money, and energy earning their degree. They also focused on a specific area of research and obtained a wealth of knowledge in that area. Now they can use that knowledge to consult. Opportunities exist for working as a freelancer or working at a consulting firm.

Individuals who want to consult immediately after obtaining their degree might find it better to work for a consulting firm to gain required experience. These firms deal with many different types of clients, and many of them actively recruit people with doctorate degree. The following is a link to various types of management consulting firms with employment potential:

http://www.consultingcase101.com/list-of-top-management-consulting-firms/

After developing an understanding of how consulting works, you will be ready to venture out as an entrepreneur. Many graduates have become owners of organizations that help other organizations thrive and survive.

Working in Industry

Contrary to what some people might believe, teaching and consulting are not the only options for using a doctoral degree. A plethora of opportunity exists in industry, and they exist in a variety of different capacities. The following are a few examples:

- Law - Law firms might be in need of doctoral level skills. You know how to conduct research, and this is a big part of the legal profession.
- Finance – You can apply quantitative skills to the financial sector. Many financial firms are in need of people who can obtain information and crunch numbers.
- Marketing – You have the ability to conduct interviews for marketing organizations. Jobs exist for qualitative researchers...you just need to find them.
- Technical Sales – Doctoral graduates are able to gather information, organize it, and accomplish a goal. This is something that technical salespeople need. Organizations recruit people who can work and think independently to represent the functionality of their products, and you have that ability.
- Writing – This is something that will come naturally. Doctoral graduates are very well suited for writing careers based on the experience they obtained in the classroom and during the writing of their dissertations.

Essentially, the potential for work is unlimited. You can work for a radio station, television station, movie production house, newspaper, magazine, academic journal, book publisher, or blogger. You can also work as a speechwriter or ghost writer for people looking for these services.

Final Thoughts

Some doctoral graduates only have one goal in mind...to work as a college professor. Remember that there are a limited number of full-time professorships available. As such, graduates may struggle to find full-time positions; and it can be difficult earning a living in an adjunct capacity. Be aware of this, and keep an open mind about all potential employment.

Upon completion of your degree, you might want to seriously consider a career outside of academia. Non-academic positions can be very rewarding, and the financial compensation may be much greater than salaries earned at universities.

Be confident and remember....when one door shuts, another door opens!

Here's to your success!